i explore

BUGS

make
believe
ideas

This book belongs to: _____

WHAT'S INSIDE?

Discover more about the amazing world of bugs!

Bees

Flies

Spiders

3-D

Throughout this book, you will find 3-D pictures to explore. Look for the 3-D glasses symbol to find them! To view the pictures, remove the 3-D glasses from the book cover and then hold the red lens over your left eye and the blue lens over your right eye. Watch as the picture comes to life!

Beetles

Butterflies

Dragonflies

True bugs

Centipedes & millipedes

i explore more & index

BEES

Class: Insects

Like all insects, bees have six legs and a body made up of three parts: a head, a thorax, and an abdomen. Some bees, like honeybees, live in a large, organized group called a colony, while others live on their own.

thorax

→ **i learn** ✕

Bees use their antennae to sense the world around them. They can smell, touch, taste, and hear through their antennae.

head

antenna

💡 **i discover**

Life in a honeybee colony involves a lot of work! The queen bee lays the eggs, the male bees mate with the queens of other colonies, and the female workers build the nest, protect the others, look for food, and care for the young!

Bees make honeycomb inside their nests – this is where young bees grow and honey is stored.

Bees defend their colony by using their stinger to inject venom into enemies, such as wasps.

wing

abdomen

leg

Honeycomb structure

Bee nest in a tree

Honeybee stinger

BEETLES

Class: Insects

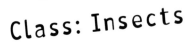
front wing

Ladybugs, dung beetles, and fireflies are all different types of beetle. There are so many types of beetle in the world that they make up a quarter of all known animals!

→ i learn ✕

Beetles are different from most insects because they have hard front wings, called wing casings, which cover and protect their back wings.

Despite its name, the firefly is actually a beetle! Under its abdomen, it has a special organ that produces light. Fireflies flash in a pattern to attract a mate. The male firefly flashes and if a female is nearby, she flashes back.

light organ

Firefly

abdomen

back wing

As their name suggests, dung beetles eat dung! They roll the dung into balls before pushing it away from the dung pile. Some dung beetles can roll balls 50 times their own weight!

The dung beetle is not the only beetle to be named after its food – the mint-leaf beetle loves to eat mint leaves!

Dung beetle

Mint-leaf beetle

BUTTERFLIES

Class: Insects

Beautiful butterflies begin their lives as caterpillars. All butterflies have two pairs of large wings and a long, straw-like tube called a proboscis, which they use to drink nectar.

antenna

proboscis

🏠 | **i facts** | 🔍

i All insects have a skeleton on the outside of their body. This skeleton protects the insect's body from injury.

If a butterfly gets too cold, it cannot move to find food or get away from attackers. Butterflies bask in the sun in order to warm up their body.

« »

Butterfly basking in the sun

A butterfly's wings are covered in tiny, overlapping scales. One side of a butterfly's wing is often brightly colored and patterned, while the other is plain and helps the butterfly to blend in to its surroundings.

wing

💡 **i discover**

A butterfly begins as an egg. The egg hatches into a caterpillar and the caterpillar eats and grows until it is ready to form a chrysalis. Inside the chrysalis, the caterpillar changes until it is ready to break out as an adult butterfly.

egg

chrysalis

A monarch caterpillar grows up

FLIES

haltere

wing

Class: Insects

Unlike dragonflies and butterflies, true flies only have one pair of wings! True flies belong to a group of insects that are called Diptera, which means two wings.

i discover

Have you ever noticed that mosquitoes bite some people more often than others? This is because mosquitoes can smell the difference between people's sweat. If they prefer the smell of your sweat, you are more likely to get bitten!

Mosquito on human skin

A fly has two halteres, which look like little stubs behind its wings. Halteres stabilize a fly when it is flying, so it is able to make quick movements in the air – this is why flies are so hard to catch!

House fly

leg

Buzzing house fly

🏠 | i facts

ⓘ House flies can taste food with their legs and feet!

○ The buzzing sound you hear when flies fly near you is actually the sound of their beating wings!

DRAGONFLIES

Class: Insects

front wing

Dragonflies get their name from their dragon-like appearance. Even though dragonflies have six legs, most of them are not very good at walking. Luckily, they are extremely fast fliers!

Fossil of a dragonfly ⊗

i facts

Dragonflies are the most ancient of all flying insects. They were even around before the dinosaurs!

Dragonflies also have a 360-degree view of the world around them, which helps them to spot prey and predators.

Large dragonfly eyes

→ **i learn** ✕

Dragonflies' wings are very flexible and fast. Dragonflies can move each of their four wings separately, changing the speed and angle to make quick movements – they can even fly backwards and hover over one spot!

eye

back wing

leg

i discover

A dragonfly's legs are covered in tiny spikes to help it catch its prey. When a dragonfly flies, it curls its legs underneath its body to form a basket shape. Small insects, like moths, are caught in this "basket" and held secure by the spikes until they are eaten.

Dragonfly eating a moth ✕

TRUE BUGS

Class: Insects

We use the word "bug" to describe most creepy crawlies, but not all creepy crawlies are actually bugs! Shield bugs and aphids are two creatures that are true bugs.

antenna

rostrum

leg

→ i learn ✕

True bugs, like this aphid, have a long, thin rostrum. Aphids use their rostrum to pierce plant stems and suck out the sugary sap. This provides them with food.

Green shield bugs are sometimes called green stink bugs. They take this name from the strong, stinky smell they release if they feel threatened.

Green shield bug

Assassin bug eating

Cicada

i facts

An Assassin bug uses its rostrum to inject other insects with toxic saliva. It then sucks out its prey's insides!

If you snap your fingers, a male cicada will follow the noise because it sounds like a female cicada!

SPIDERS

Class: Arachnids

All arachnids have eight legs –
this includes animals like
scorpions, harvestmen,
and, most commonly, spiders!
Unlike insects, an arachnid
has no antennae.

Leg

i facts

i

Harvestmen look similar to spiders,
but unlike spiders, they cannot
produce any silk.

The smallest-known spider
measured 0.02 in (0.43 mm) –
that's smaller than a pinhead!

Harvestman

All spiders can produce silk, but they do not always use it to catch their prey. Some spiders make nests out of silk, and others use it to help them climb. Some spiders even use their silk as a parachute.

two body segments

Spider's silk nest

chelicerae

fang

i learn

Despite the tarantula's scary appearance, its venom is actually less dangerous than a bee's sting! Like all spiders, tarantulas have chelicerae, which they use to grasp and hold their prey while they bite and inject venom into it.

CENTIPEDES AND MILLIPEDES

Class: Myriapods

Centipedes and millipedes are myriapods. "Myriad" means many or countless. Some myriapods have 10 legs, while others have up to 750! A myriapod's long body is made of many segments.

sensory bristles

Millipede's segmented body

i facts

i Millipedes have two pairs of legs for every segment of their body, whereas centipedes only have one pair.

Millipedes have brush-like hairs on their second and third pair of legs, which they use to clean their antennae.

Antennae feeling the ground ⊗

« »

→ i learn ⊗

Centipedes can walk backwards or forwards. Their antennae feel the ground as they move forwards, while their back legs have special hairs, called sensory bristles, which help them to feel their way around if they move backwards.

💡 i discover

When a centipede loses a leg, it grows another to replace it.

centipede

head

segmented body

leg

antenna

Some spiders use their silk like a balloon to fly over huge distances. Spiders can balloon as high as 16,000 ft (4,877 m), which is high enough to fly over parts of the Himalayas!

Ancient Egyptians thought that the Earth was a big ball of dung that was pushed around by a dung beetle. They painted their god, Khepera, as a dung beetle.

Insects make up almost half of the world's species.

The fastest beetle is the Australian tiger beetle. It can run up to 5.5 mph (9 kph).

Some ancient dragonflies had a wingspan of up to 2 ft (60 cm)!

The praying mantis can turn its head round to look right behind itself. This makes it very good at spotting prey.